WHY
WE ARE
BAPTIZED

WHY WE ARE BAPTIZED

KATHY ENGLAND

Illustrated by Julie Fuhriman Young

Deseret Book Company
Salt Lake City, Utah
1981

First printing August 1978
Second printing January 1981
Third printing May 1982
Fourth printing March 1983
Fifth printing November 1984
Sixth printing July 1985
Seventh printing May 1986
Eighth printing November 1988

Library of Congress Cataloging in Publication Data

England, Kathy, 1954–
    Why we are baptized.

    SUMMARY: Explains the administering of baptism and
how it can affect your life.
        1. Baptism—Mormonism—Juvenile literature.
[1. Baptism—Mormonism.   2. Church of Jesus Christ of
Latter-day Saints.   3. Mormons and Mormonism]
I. Title.
BX8655.3.E53   234'.161   78-19180
ISBN 0-87747-893-7

When you are eight years old you will be ready to be baptized. Usually your family will go with you to a place where there is enough water for your baptism— a river, a lake, a swimming pool, or a baptismal font. Dressed all in white, you will be helped into the water by the man who will baptize you. This man, who will also be dressed in white, may be your father or someone else who has the authority and power to baptize. This power and authority, called the priesthood, was given through Jesus Christ.

2

When you are standing in the water with the man who will baptize you, he will hold you by the wrist and you will hold onto his arm. Then he will raise his right arm to form a half square. He will call you by name and say, "Having been commissioned of Jesus Christ, I baptize you in the name of the Father, and of the Son, and of the Holy Ghost. Amen."

Now he may tell you quietly to relax and hold your breath for just a few seconds until you come up out of the water again. When you are ready, he will hold you carefully and gently immerse (completely cover) you in the water.

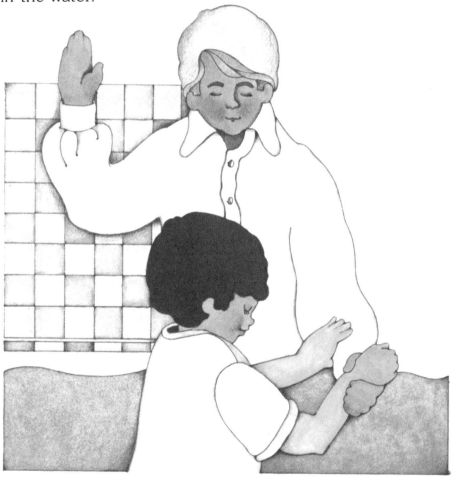

When you come up out of the water, everyone there will be happy that you chose to be baptized. They will probably smile to show that they love you. Then the man who has baptized you will help you out of the water so you can go to a dressing room and change into dry clothes. When you are dry and warm and dressed again, you will be greeted by your happy family and friends.

But you will be different—different in a very special way!

4 ow will I be different?" you ask. That is a good question. There is much more for you to learn about being baptized than just how it is done. Even more important is to understand *why* and *how* baptism can change your whole life.

Before we were born, we lived with our Father in heaven. We wanted to come to earth so we could learn how to become more like Him. When we chose to come to earth, we knew life would be exciting and fun, but we also knew that it would not always be easy to do what is right. However, our Father promised that if we did, then we could return and live with Him forever. But if we chose to do the things that our Heavenly Father did not want us to do, then we would not be able to live with Him again.

6   We wanted very much to return to our Father because He loves us so dearly. We also knew we would be happy with Him because of our love for Him. We were excited to know we would have freedom to choose how we would live on earth. There we could show our love for our Father in heaven by doing what He has asked all of His children to do.

Our Father told us that we would not remember living with Him. But He promised to send His Son, Jesus Christ, to teach us all that we must do to live with Him again.

8 Our Heavenly Father knew that sometimes we might make wrong choices. However, He will forgive us if we fully repent when we do wrong. Then we must tell Him that we are sorry, and promise not to make that wrong choice again.

Jesus, who is our Elder Brother, offered to be punished for us if we repent of any wrongdoing and believe in Him. Because He loves us so much, He let Himself be nailed to a cross of wood and crucified. He died as punishment for the sins (wrong choices) of all of our Heavenly Father's children so that they might have an opportunity to live again with our Father in heaven.

10   Jesus lived almost two thousand years ago. There are many wonderful stories in the Bible and the Book of Mormon that show His love for us and for our Heavenly Father. Jesus especially loved children.

Jesus wants everyone to make the right choices. He obeyed our Father in all ways and taught many people about Him.

If we wisely follow the example of Jesus' goodness and kindness, we will be able to return to our Heavenly Father just as He promised.

When Jesus lived on earth He was baptized by immersion in the river Jordan, in obedience to one of our Heavenly Father's important commandments and to make it possible for Him to return and live with Heavenly Father.

Baptism is like taking the first step on a long journey home. When Jesus was baptized, he showed us how to begin our journey back to the presence of our Father in heaven.

12 Even though He was perfect, Jesus was baptized by immersion just as all people must be to become members of The Church of Jesus Christ of Latter-day Saints. When we are baptized, we are following Jesus' example and we take upon ourselves the name of Christ. Then we should always try to live just as Jesus lived.

Membership in The Church of Jesus Christ of Latter-day Saints is a wonderful blessing. It makes it possible for us to take the first step on the road back to the presence of our Heavenly Father.

14 Jesus taught that we must be eight years old before we are baptized, because we need to be old enough to know how to make choices that will please our Father in heaven, and how to repent if we make a wrong choice.

When we are old enough to understand how to make right choices and how to repent, then we are accountable (responsible); we have reached the age of accountability.

Many people do not know about The Church of Jesus Christ of Latter-day Saints. Sometimes they do not want to become members until they are over eight years of age.

You are blessed because you already know what you must do to live again with our Father in heaven.

16 After you are baptized, you will be given a special gift and blessing by priesthood holders. They will lay their hands upon your head and confirm you a member of The Church of Jesus Christ of Latter-day Saints and command you to receive the Holy Ghost.

Now you are a follower of Jesus Christ!

Before leaving this earth to return to our Father in heaven, the Savior promised His followers that the Holy Ghost would help them to make right choices and would also be their Comforter.

Listening to the Holy Ghost helps us to know what our Father in heaven wants us to do.
Listen for the promptings of the Spirit when you pray for help in making right choices. If you have a good and comforting feeling, it means you have made the right choice. If you feel confused or upset, then you have not made the right choice and you will need to think about it and pray for more guidance.

Receiving the Holy Ghost is called the baptism of the Spirit. Sometimes it is also called baptism by fire because the special feeling that comes is like a burning in our chest. The Holy Ghost bears testimony to us that Jesus Christ lives and loves us.

20 As we learn about the life of Jesus and try to follow His example, we will know that what the Holy Ghost tells us is true. The Holy Ghost will help us to know everything that we must do to return to our Father in heaven.

Every Sunday in church meetings we partake of the sacrament. The sacrament blessings promise that if we will remember the Savior and keep His commandments, we will always have His Spirit to be with us. Partaking of the sacrament helps us to always remember Jesus Christ and to truly try to follow Him in all that we do.

22 When you understand why you must be baptized, you will know and be grateful for your baptism as one of the most important events of your whole life.

Our Heavenly Father loves you very much. He wants you to return to Him. He will always bless you and help you if you try to do what is right.

Your baptism is just the beginning, your first step on the way home to live with Him again.

24

Page 2
Doctrine and Covenants 20:72–74

"Baptism is to be administered in the following manner unto all those who repent—The person who is called of God and has authority from Jesus Christ to baptize, shall go down into the water with the person who has presented himself or herself for baptism, and shall say, calling him or her by name: Having been commissioned of Jesus Christ, I baptize you in the name of the Father, and of the Son, and of the Holy Ghost. Amen. Then shall he immerse him or her in the water, and come forth again out of the water."

Page 6
John 14:15

"If ye love me, keep my commandments."

Page 7
John 3:16

"For God so loved the world, that he gave his only begotten Son, that whosoever believeth in him should not perish, but have everlasting life."

Page 8
Doctrine and Covenants 1:32

"Nevertheless, he that repents and does the commandments of the Lord shall be forgiven."

Page 9
1 Thessalonians 5:9–10

"Our Lord Jesus Christ…died for us, that…we should live together with him."

Page 11
Mark 1:9–11

"And it came to pass in those days, that Jesus came from Nazareth of Galilee, and was baptized of John in Jordan.

And straightway coming up out of the water, he saw the **25**
heavens opened, and the Spirit like a dove descending
upon him: And there came a voice from heaven, saying,
Thou art my beloved Son, in whom I am well pleased."

Page 12
Doctrine and Covenants 20:37

*"And again, by way of commandment to the church
concerning the manner of baptism*—All those who humble
themselves before God, and desire to be baptized, and
come forth…and are willing to take upon them the name
of Jesus Christ, having a determination to serve him
to the end, and truly manifest by their works that they
have received of the Spirit of Christ…shall be received by
baptism into his church."

Page 13
Mosiah 18:7–10

"And it came to pass after many days there were a goodly
number gathered together at the place of Mormon, to
hear the words of Alma….He said unto them: Behold, here
are the waters of Mormon…and now, as ye are desirous
to come into the fold of God, and to be called his people,
and are willing to bear one another's burdens, that they
may be light; Yea, and are willing to mourn with those that
mourn; yea, and comfort those that stand in need of
comfort, and to stand as witnesses of God at all times and
in all things, and in all places that ye may be in, even until
death, that ye may be redeemed of God, and be
numbered with those of the first resurrection, that ye may
have eternal life—Now I say unto you, if this be the desire
of your hearts, what have you against being baptized in
the name of the Lord, as a witness before him that ye
have entered into a covenant with him, that ye will serve
him and keep his commandments, that he may pour out
his Spirit more abundantly upon you?"

26

Page 14
Doctrine and Covenants 20:71

"No one can be received into the church of Christ unless he has arrived unto the years of accountability before God, and is capable of repentance."

Page 15
Doctrine and Covenants 18:42

"For all men must repent and be baptized, and not only men, but women, and children who have arrived at the years of accountability."

Page 16
Article of Faith 4

"We believe that the first principles and ordinances of the Gospel are: first, Faith in the Lord Jesus Christ; second, Repentance; third, Baptism by immersion for the remission of sins; fourth, Laying on of hands for the gift of the Holy Ghost."

Page 17
John 14:16, 26

"And I will pray the Father, and he shall give you another Comforter, that he may abide with you for ever....The Comforter, which is the Holy Ghost, whom the Father will send in my name, he shall teach you all things, and bring all things to your remembrance, whatsoever I have said unto you."

Page 18
Doctrine and Covenants 9:8–9

"But, behold, I say unto you, that you must study it out in your mind; then you must ask me if it be right, and if it is right I will cause that your bosom shall burn within you; therefore, you shall feel that it is right. But if it be not right you shall have no such feelings."

Page 19
2 Nephi 31:13

"I know that if ye shall follow the Son, with full purpose of heart,...repenting of your sins, witnessing unto the Father that ye are willing to take upon you the name of Christ, by baptism—yea, by following your Lord and your Savior down into the water, according to his word, behold, then shall ye receive the Holy Ghost; yea, then cometh the baptism of fire and of the Holy Ghost."

Page 20
2 Nephi 32:5

"For behold, again I say unto you that if ye will enter in by the way, and receive the Holy Ghost, it will show unto you all things what ye should do."

Page 21
Doctrine and Covenants 20:77

"O God, the Eternal Father, we ask thee in the name of thy Son, Jesus Christ, to bless and sanctify this bread to the souls of all those who partake of it, that they may eat in remembrance of the body of thy Son, and witness unto thee, O God, the Eternal Father, that they are willing to take upon them the name of thy Son, and always remember him and keep his commandments which he has given them; that they may always have his Spirit to be with them. Amen."

Page 22
2 Nephi 31:17, 20

"For the gate by which ye should enter is repentance and baptism by water....Wherefore, ye must press forward with a steadfastness in Christ, having a perfect brightness of hope, and a love of God and of all men. Wherefore, if ye shall press forward, feasting upon the word of Christ, and endure to the end, behold thus saith the Father: Ye shall have eternal life."